From The Best Selling Children's First Questions Series

What are the Signs of Allah?

by Emma Apple

Rewritten and republished in full color for the 5th Anniversary of the series.

Words and Illustrations Copyright © 2020 Emma Apple

All rights reserved. This book or any portion thereof may not be reproduced or used in any manner without the express written permission of the copyright holder.

Published by Little Moon Books
First Published 2017 under the title Is Allah Real?

Second Edition
Paperback

ISBN-13: 978-0-9951323-6-8

www.littlemoonbooks.com

What are the Signs of Allah?

Bismillah ar-Rahman ar-Rahim
With God's name.

The aim of this book is to encourage children to look at the natural world and think about how Allah created it and the signs of Allah around them.

We hope that this will help children and their families to know their creator and to look closer at the natural world to understand Him.

The way sunflower seeds are perfectly placed on the flower and leaves branch out on just the right angle.

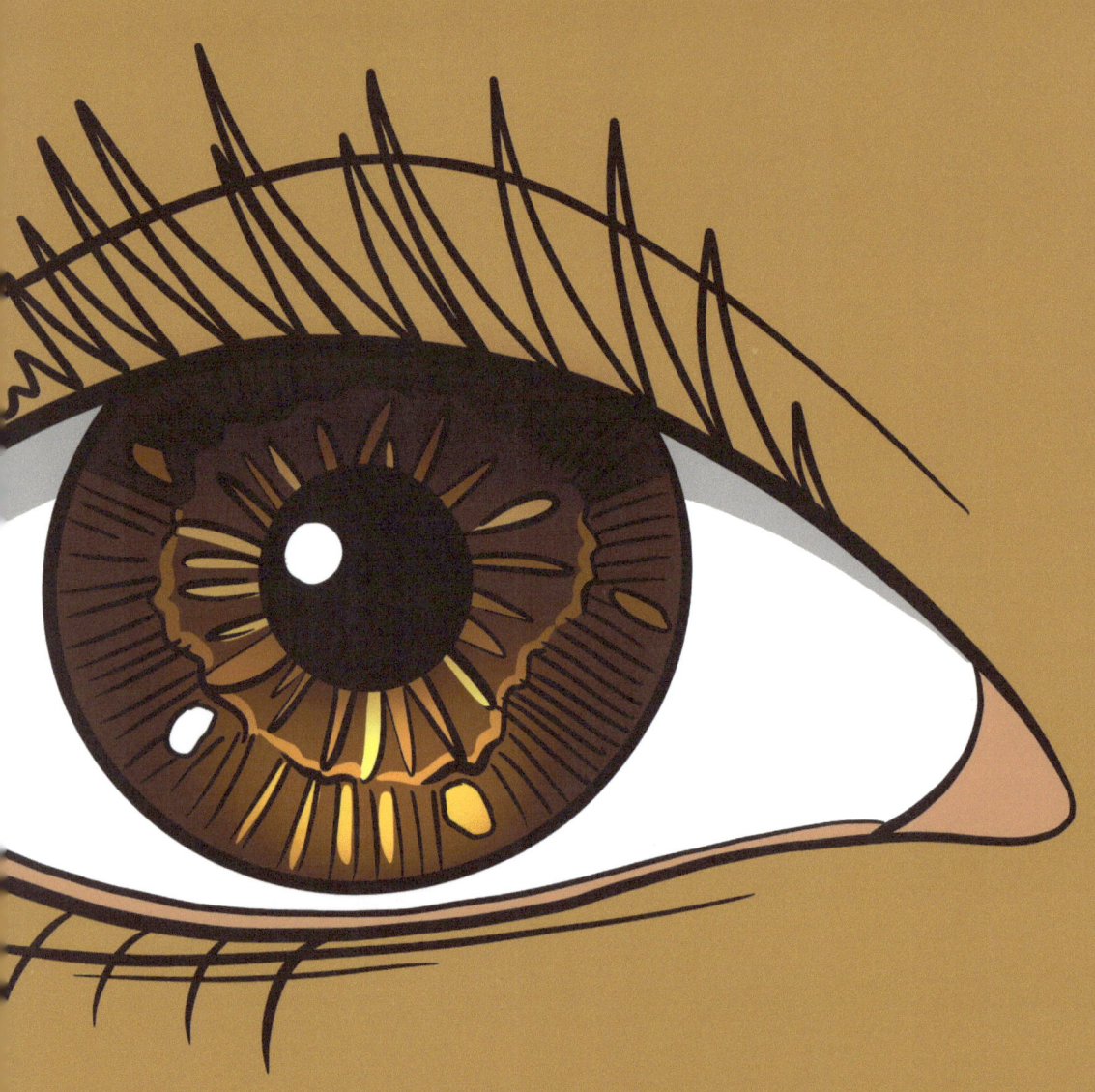

The human brain was made to look for patterns.

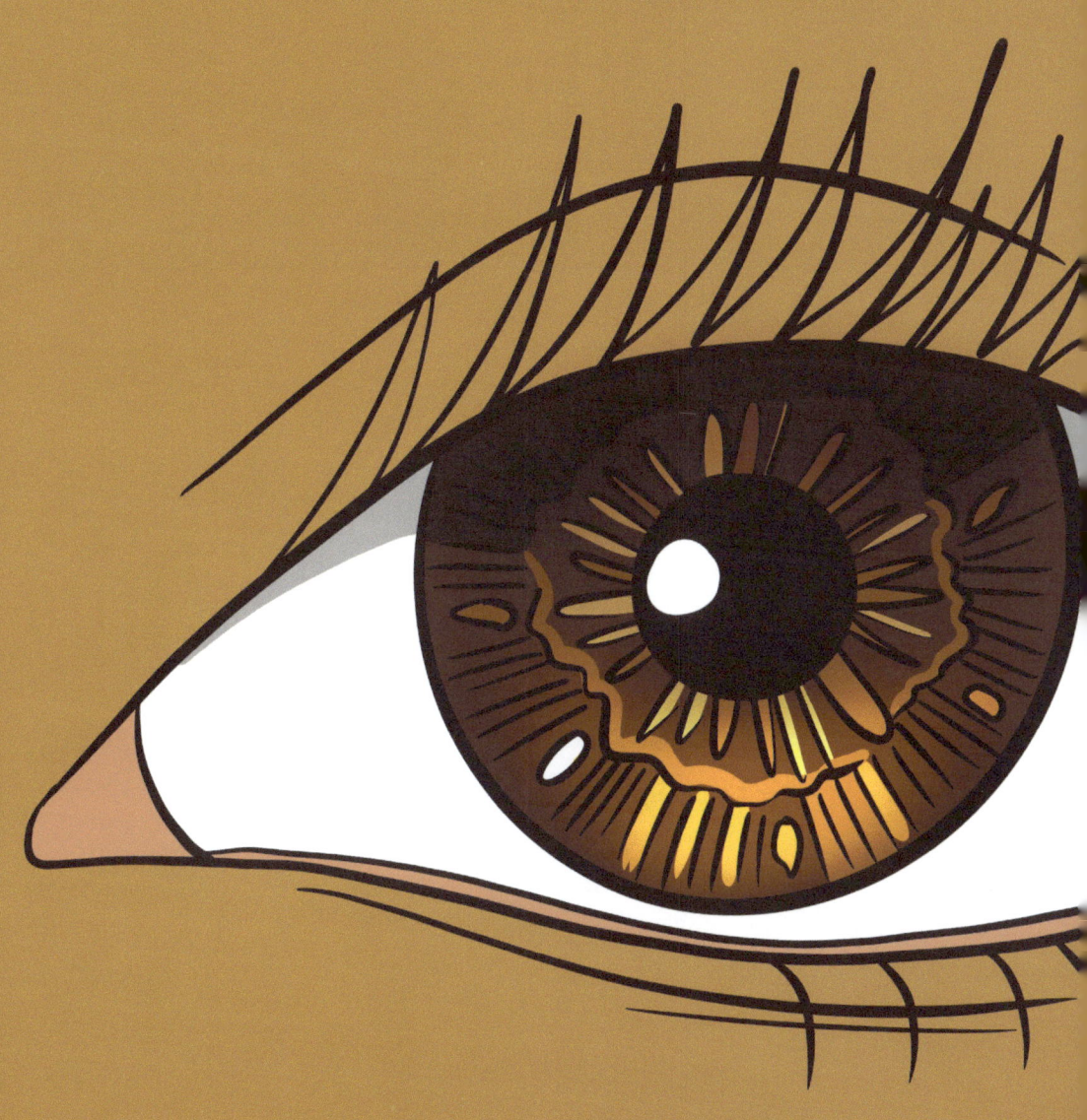

We see them and use them all over and beyond our world.

In art

In the human body

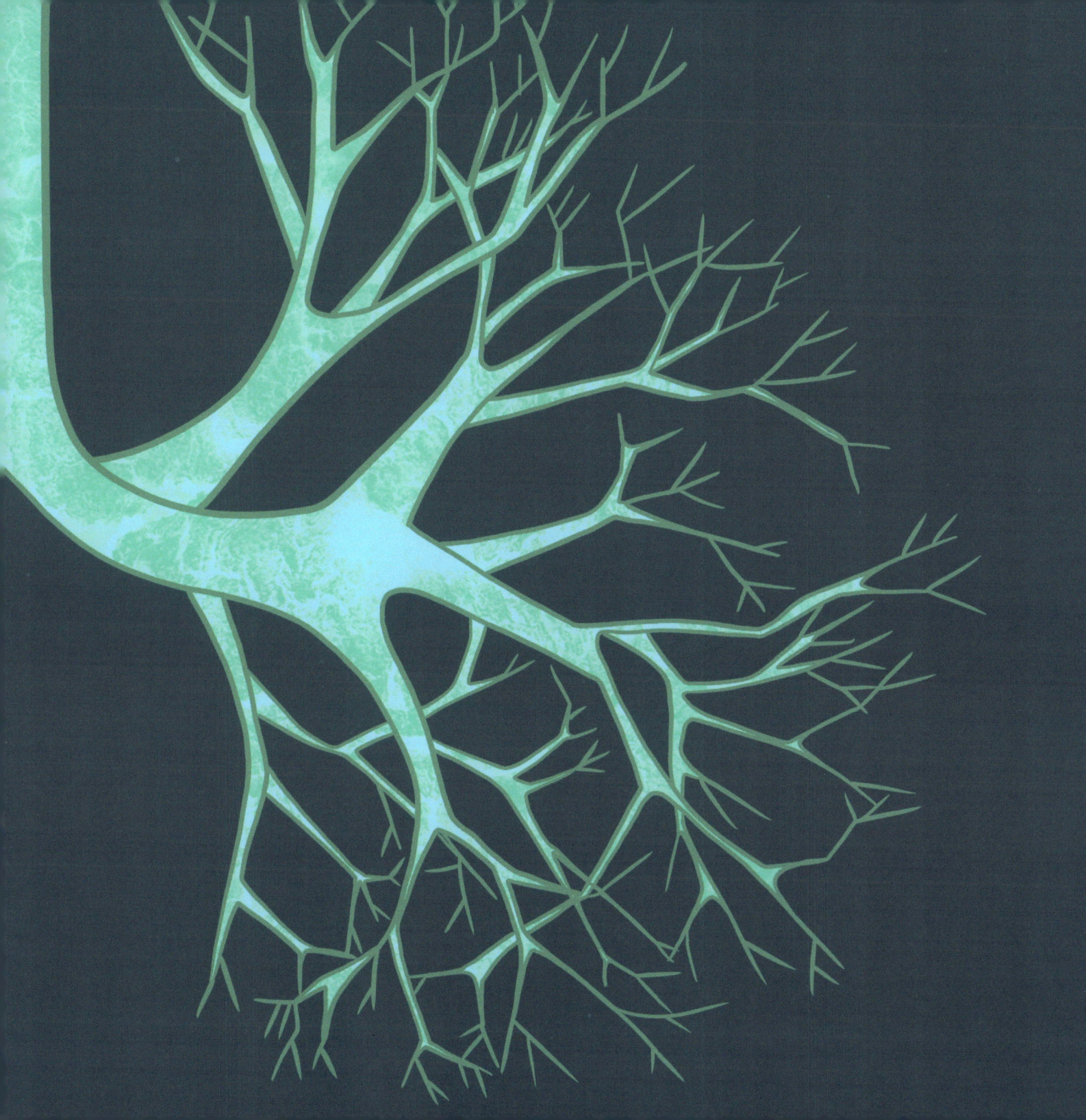

In nature.

Similar patterns are found

all

throughout

the universe

We find them in the most unexpected places.

Plants and our own lungs use repeating fractal patterns.

Beautiful symmetry is found on faces, insect and animal markings, in flowers, and all through nature.

Repeating tessellation is seen in honeycombs, scales, and rock formations.

Weather patterns, shells, and some galaxies,
are formed in a spiral.

We humans also use these patterns in art, design, architecture, and in many other ways.

The natural world is adorned by patterns such as these that seem to balance everything in a divine order.

Allah made us so that we would look for patterns in nature, and recognize them as His signs.

We can't detect Allah with our senses, but we can see His presence and touch in the balance and order of His creation.

"And He it is Who spread the earth and placed mountains and streams in it and inserted in it two pairs of the each kind of fruit. He covers the day with the night. Certainly, there are signs in these matters for a people who reflect."

Qur'an Ar-Ra'd 3

Answering Questions with The Scientific Method

The Scientific Method is the way that scientists answer a question or begin to solve a problem or answer a question.

You can use it too! This is how it works:

1. Ask a question and research the answer. Look online, read books, talk to teachers and experts. Gather as many facts as you can that will help you in your search for the answer.

2. Form a hypothesis (an educated guess). Based on your research, predict what the answer to your question could be.

3. Test it! Design some tests or experiments for finding out if your hypothesis is correct.

4. Collect and analyze data (information). Write down everything that happened during your experiments. Look for patterns.

5. Form a conclusion. Look at all the data you've collected and figure out if your hypothesis was correct, and why or why not.

6. Communicate what you found. Share what you discovered so other scientists can learn from, test, or build on what you learned.

Glossary

Real - Something that exists and is not imaginary.

Architecture - The design, style, and action of creating a building.

Fractal - A complex geometric pattern that repeats the same shape at smaller and smaller sizes.

Symmetry - Something that is the same on opposite sides.

Tesselation - The same shape repeated in a mosaic or checkered pattern.

Spiral - A line that curves around and out from the center.

Divine - Relating to God.

Detect - To discover the existence of something.

Senses - Things we use to perceive something, such as sight, hearing, touch, taste, smell, movement.

The Children's First Questions series promotes curiosity and encourages the pursuit of knowledge, and scientific literacy.

Helping children to grasp complex concepts in a unique and age appropriate way, using authentic Islamic sources and scientific facts.

Other books in the Children's First Questions Series

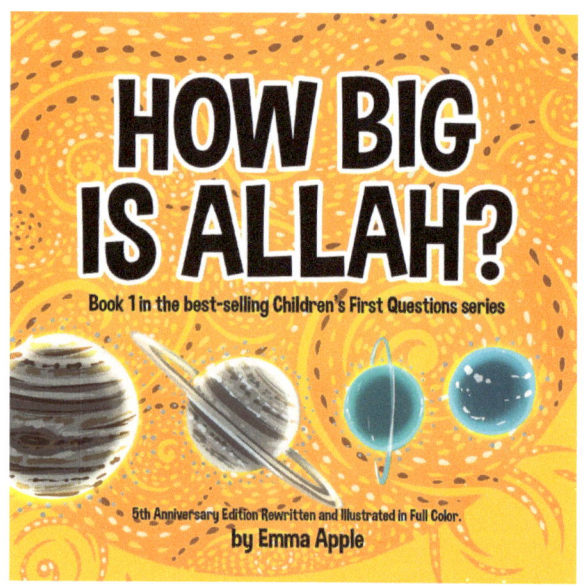
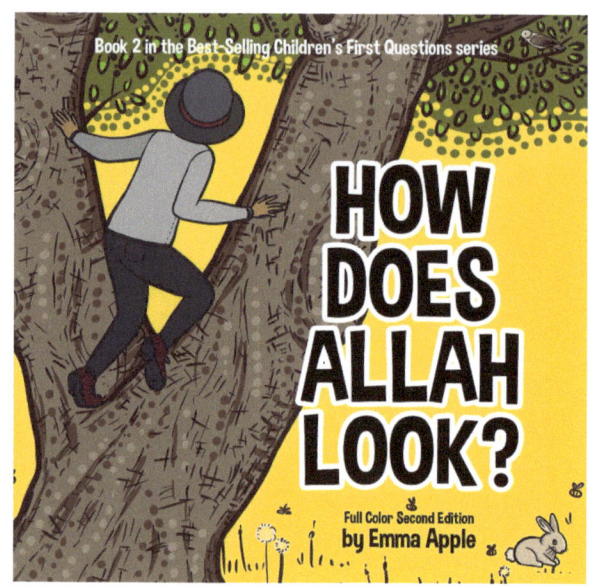
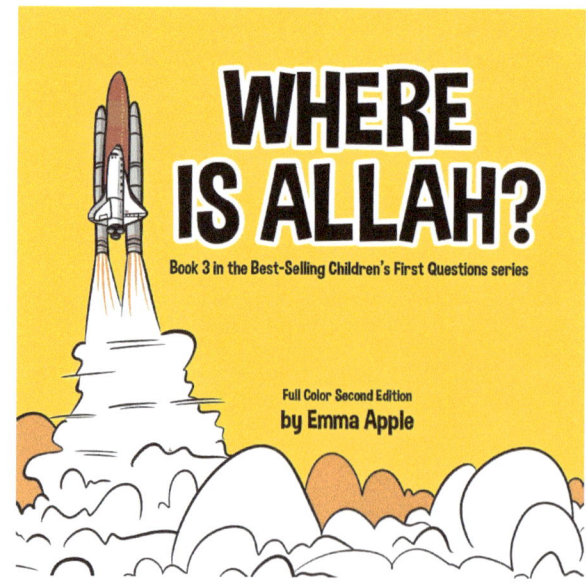

More from Little Moon Books

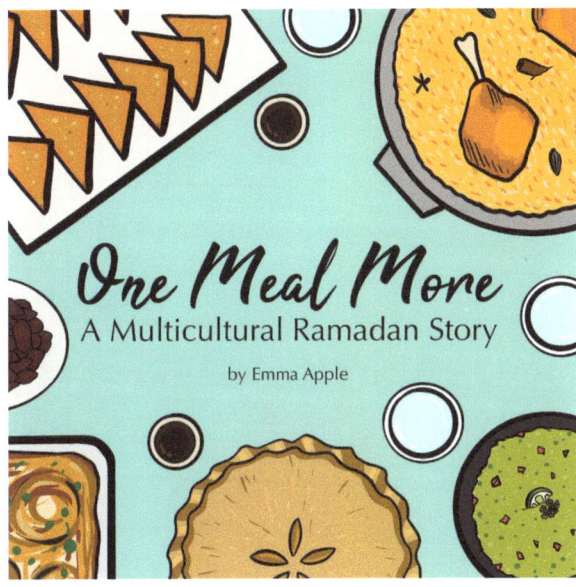

littlemoonbooks.com

www.ingramcontent.com/pod-product-compliance
Lightning Source LLC
LaVergne TN
LVHW071027070426
835507LV00002B/51